living must bury

JOSIE SIGLER

Book layout by   Colie Collen
Book design by   Fence Books

Published in the United States by   Fence Books
                                        Science Library 320
                                        University at Albany
                                        1400 Washington Avenue
                                        Albany, NY 12222
                                        www.fenceportal.org

Fence Books are distributed by   University Press of New England
                                        www.upne.com

and printed in Canada by   Westcan Printing Group
                                        www.westcanpg.com

Library of Congress Cataloguing in Publication Data
        Sigler, Josie [1976–]
        Living Must Bury/ Josie Sigler

Library of Congress Control Number: 2010923757

ISBN 1-934200-36-0
ISBN 13:978-1-934200-36-0

FIRST EDITION
10 9 8 7 6 5 4 3 2

FENCE BOOKS are published in partnership with the University at Albany and
the New York State Writers Institute, and with help from the New York State
Council on the Arts, the National Endowment for the Arts, and the friends of
Fence.

living must bury

JOSIE SIGLER

THE 2010 MOTHERWELL PRIZE

FENCE
BOOKS

ALBANY, NEW YORK

For Dorothy

Acknowledgments

Published in *Night Train*: "O You with a Spine," "those who leave their scent on cloth," "those who dream entirely in Matisses," "those who curse horses," and "O those shipfitters who dream" (as "The Shipfitter Dreams").

Published in *Pebble Lake Review*: "Yes, those who fail to read guides & fall in love."

Published in *Calamity*, (Proem Press, chapbook): "Living Must Bury."

Thank you Jennifer, always, for being my love and my light, for your continual willingness to dig into the hard stuff with me and the way we laugh together, too.

Thanks to Benjamin Shockey, who gave me the idea for this book, and who, instead of interrupting, dusted around me while I wrote the first draft in our living room near the Pacific and made me many cups of tea.

Thanks to Cody Todd, Saba Razvi, Kelli Anne Noftle, Tabitha Morgan, Rachel Moritz, Jessica Piazza, and David St. John, who read early versions of these poems with love.

Thanks to Janalynn Bliss, who told me to send the book to *Fence* and loaned me change for postage.

Thanks to Rebecca Wolff, for recognizing these poems in their wilderness and for being so real. Thanks to Colie for making the poems on the page look like the ones in my head.

Thanks to Catherine Ratliff, for conversation and giving me the hills of South Dakota, both of which healed me.

Thank you Jeremy, Jeanne, Mom and Dad. Without you, nothing.

*If there is [a universe], we must conjecture its purpose; we must
conjecture the words, the definitions, the etymologies, the synonyms,
from the secret dictionary of God.*

—Jorge Luis Borges
El idioma analítico de John Wilkins

*I shall bury the wounded like pupas,
I shall count and bury the dead.*

—Sylvia Plath
"Getting There"

Contents

27......................*those who shimmer in corn spell, those with hearts* wide as watermelons, those who know me, those who listen with ears made of conch shells, those for whom denim pants are atrocity, those feral children. those isolated, those Dryads, those suffering Kaspar Hauser Syndrome, psychosocial dwarfism, mistakenly understood as failure-to-thrive. those the wolves sing to sleep. those monsters of sorts, those coming in the fury of love, those licked & bathed by such tongues. those children imprisoned by Emperor Frederick II.

31..........*those who covet the bridges in other cities,* those shivering on the deck, those who were once stars. those for whom crumbling is not an instant's act, a fundamental pause, those who understand diatomaceous earth, those who seem, in the dark passageway, like they cannot comprehend scars. those who know every sale is an amputation. those who can't sell & lose limbs anyway. those who take up the thick knot & count protrusions. those who whisper. those for whom single mausolea may be permanently sealed. those for whom consecutive & slow. those who long to be anywhere, anywhere else.

those animals insane for the destination, those who cannot pause at the horizon. those who are sockets, those who know rain, so long in coming, softens husks of corn. those who crack eggs at a table once used for the slaughter. those who have no other choice, those who croon, those out of work, those in an abandoned boxcar. those who hold what can never die nor reach the border..33

35......................*those who frequent carnivals,* caught in the rings of Saturn. those who are the product of a sour meeting between egg & sperm— those who would do you no harm, lamb, duckling, turtle, dove. those who play tennis with spatulas & balloons, (those who pray for an elephant to swallow them), those who plug their ears in ancient buildings, those who avoid pleas & moans coming through the pipes & toilets. those who are prison-broken, those who allow themselves to be lifted in expatriate arms, earn pink wisps *that melt on the tongue. those who ride the spinning ride, those who cry when the floor drops out, those who will never come clean, those who have become boys protecting their mother, those who walk on the map of Jupiter, those freaks.*

those dallying, dallying, wanting to go in, those..................................39
fruit flies on the edge of a wineglass, those who would be happy to die. those cellmates gathered around such weeping, those for whom double-jeopardy, those pleas substantiated. those who free us from the binds we wanted.

40..**living must bury**

42............................**those who cannot reverse the damage of Armstrong's boots,** *those barn cats having escaped fire, those who look over their shoulder at every dry-grass crackle. those who sat in church at seven years old screaming prayer, those orgasms pulled from the center, long chain of vowels, those who take only the tusks, leaving behind the burden of flesh, the grey & wrinkled hide—those without scars to recall the wound, those trophies, those beating their tailfins against the headlines.*

those who hail semis, those seers, those canaries *blinded by lightning, those who start singing at midnight. those who find they survived. those for whom the future sings even when it's gone blank. those who did not come through, those for whom the body is the same God they imagined as children*...45

49...**O You with a Spine**

51................................**glorious, those excavators, hands that speak,** *those who will not. Go. those who fail to save themselves. those off course, those well past.*

53.........**those who dream in Matisses, those who travel** *deep in the body & find a solitary color, those beyond religion. those leaving port, those with hankies pressed over their mouths, those hiding in the coalbin, those who are told* by history there is a possibility of escape. those who realize the ocean is a body. those who looked over the Badlands & prayed the horses could make it. those who remember the mountains shifting, their faces before the surgeons came in. those who see the nameless form of a woman & love her in the morning, arm beneath a pillow, arching.

yes, those who fail to read guides & fall in love with a woman's touch. those who rise singing from their dens. those who live underground for long hours & are reborn & say a fleet of ships is the loveliest sight on this dark earth. those who moan as they nest in windows above the street, those mermaids in heat, those who come into the room & see they've left themselves in the sheets & must return to that hollow. those included in the present classification & those sundry, those who know what miracles birds know...55

those gathering the dust of the earth on fence posts, those driving from Oklahoma, those last leaves that cling to the tree through January. those stars whose light might still be visible, those who climbed to the bottom of the old well to press their heads against the cool walls. those who evidence the violence done between souls...60

those who curse horses, who repeatedly fail to tithe,

those who come from the river Lethe hulled with such knives.
those who kill the animals that want to die. Such culling

calls me further, ladle to mouth that I might transmigrate
with no remembrance of the largess on the map of Jupiter,

hurricane of blood & the red wolf's profile, too, an erasure
in the Tennessee hills until evidence of fossil & bounty.

1768, gifted in return for the kill, field of gold tobacco
& the problem of hope—Our spines searched nascent

seams in the night until they fit notch by notch. I stood
before the row of headstones, each the size of a dictionary:

those who never suckle. those who mate for life. those given
to pacing. those who turn their faces to the sky & howl.

those who leave their scent on cloth,

those who are peccable, those chaste & wise.
For example, the pelican tearing her breast

to bring her young to life with her own blood,
a living representation of Jesus. As in millinery,

let us leave the washstand choked with beauty,
rain in our gullets, the laundry. How after

we've decided on incompatibility & lack
the fucking is so sweet, the sleep in which

forgiveness grows out before me like snow-
melt in the fields of yellow. How research,

the assumption a woman in a distant time
can picture our mourning. Wanton girl,

my mother, wakes in a motel room, 1975,
as in: 1) year of the first predicted quake or

2) the invasion of East Timor. And I grow,
doubling, quadrupling in Florida's heat

& seismic hazard, the whole trembling flock
cupped as you might my breast, after all.

But you are a rusted plow, a stone half-buried.
How easily we turn the sacred into a token.

Your shirt thrown over the line was a trench
in this ocean. And I trembled when I smelled

the pelt of your chest there, the Ghost Dance,

those escapees, those deserters. those who remain
in the barracks, pressing their fingers to the wall—

The dragonflies, too, leave their translucent skins.

those who weep as they learn to walk again,

find the word for mother. Language, mere sheath, the petal
of indian pipe curled, hint of bone sounding any message.

Cord looped around my neck as if the universe remembered
the passages, too, in the tiny shaft of a feather. And Galileo,

whose same sun ripened a bunch of grapes as if it had naught
but to focus on the hangman's terror. As in belts & light zones

between & how to flee that procurance. Birth is shipwreck,
clinging to the boat her breast in my mouth, a small figurine

that fits inside another & another. Opening she'll find me
at last, so blurred, so bewildered my hands sans fingers, pin-

prick eyes, ears unfunneled, sex unhooved. But include here

those ungulates used as bait, those for whom systemic overviews
reveal a merely cursory enchantment with survival. Sans pigment,

known as the corpse plant. Or, harkens a colonial impulse.
The carnival where reverse osmosis, liquids express permanence,

river charted by ferris wheel lights, linger of fried dough.

those who stand in tears amid the alien corn,

those who wade through. Hunger season again & blue shadows between the blades of yellowed grass. As if the segregation

of color the cause of such hollow. To say the node of hunger, not, per se, 1) a knot, protuberance, but 2) a centering point

of component parts. She flew away & a wall grew around her leaving. This is what happens when last year's grain is eaten.

O those swallowing fresh knots of snow, those kleptomaniac priests

who give crucifixes from the altars they have traveled, their sexes untouched.

Come unto me, now. I have been waiting. Since the red O

appeared on the white backdrop of the sheet

certain but warm,

As if Leonardo himself had come, saying to the child: *This is the O,*

Nothing but an empty, nothing but legs & arms spread fully.

And after the small house in the body is evacuated,
what have we left?

Naught but men who brandish spears—

those who are members of the same army, those

*who breathe underwater. who stand elbow to elbow surrounded
by the dead & wounded in the trenches.* Even without the bars

between us, recognition of scent & scar, the myopia that comes
of longing. As in linoleum, which is to say: alternate uses for

burlap, camouflage, 3) mimicry, what she might ransom
& what's hidden. The long history of her body I discover

with my hungry fingers, the biological process of wound repair,
derivative of the Greek eschara, meaning fireplace. The oven

sealed where the rib once flexed. The surgeons who wrenched
it from her back like a lever & let the fulcrum of my mouth,

[O let the fulcrum *I have been waiting* O rising to the sky

Come unto me, now, here, in the dusty barracks.

I brandish bone. I am howling—

Those who long for ritual, for couplets. Those invincible. Those who
strip their clothes in the hills to wander a mountain lion's killing path

where each buffalo is more decayed than the last I walk to my death,
bitten by flies. Crouch, remove *costae fluitantes*, that which floats.

Come untethered at the insistence of her body,
zoned as peninsula, surrounded on three sides by sea.

I will break the lion's windpipe if I must. I will not
fill my pockets with stones & wade in,

[But O *let the fulcrum of my* O

let me mountain lion you

& give me territory—

[O *Come unto me—*

Bring the sun to dry ghosts on the battlefield, to euphonize
those who bleat their fury in the open fields we once adorned.

those who are infidels, who in summer once

turned wide circles in grass. Animals real & make believe,
a throw-away Jesus. She leans over our neighbor's body,

a shaft with forgiveness stitched in its seams, mouths.
And comes my alphabet. Those before me are

letters which correspond to sounds. This bitterness,
choke, feral city of 1,000 & 1,000 factories lighting up

the wide darkness over a bridge that never leads the way
out. Throat, porcelain tube twirling in night dances

of suffocation & I woke with the jury: To her in the bed?
Him on the couch? As in the alphabet opens & bends.

And my aunt's neck when her braid caught in the auger,
wound like the woman trapped in a tower with nothing

but a wheel to spin gold & her own crushed jawbone,

yes, those who would be skewered like hogs if they failed.

those who covet coral,

those in the cold housing tract
curled around the wide·blue

photograph seen once, pre-
cognition. As in feet turn

to fins, or 5) an aerodynamo.
My mother's boy who dreams

in reefs for six years the body
can no longer exist without

those of undulating pink, those
for whom the nail bed gleams.

Rock fissure or red sneaker.
Daffodil petals on cement.

Grape like they try to sell
for purple or fag's lavender,

those in mausoleums, no, those
green as a thousand moons

through the grass in the cracks
of vacant lots, robin singing

his endless call in the dark,
traffic having obscured his

desperate need to mate—

those who gotta get their hands on,
those who cannot live without.

The teacher says, *Soon, soon.*
Those with power can never

understand hunger. *(those*
who will discover trace amounts

of urine in their Mountain Dew.)
Yes, this boy knows all the tricks.

Walks in the snare drum claps,
boom bass, row of broken

palaces, the steel factory's glass,
the splinter of tracks, curvature

of dialect, already, specific to

those who won't stay mad for keeps.

those victims of freshwater lies,

those who are loud & get no lunch
& she says the beer is what keeps

her thin. Balling the jack is the
cure. And why must you X?

those fighting causes they disbelieve,
the radiant tackle in this river

as I first took breath between
her parting thighs

& my father's
boat between the two canals—

those bridges which join & separate,
as in the Congo, it's water-starved

fragments—

Let this be the pattern
for dresses worn after rape. Let a

man catch sea birds & encircle
their necks so they cannot swallow

the sweet flesh of fish. Enslave them
to him & let them turn their beaks

piteously into the sand at the end
of days. Let infants weep in their

cribs. Do not go to them. Let them
drool on plastic mattresses in wards

& daycares. Let sport be for blood.
Let the work day be long. Let them

forget the hours in which they used
to brush the flanks of horses, knit.

Let them bomb mosques, temples,
churches. Let sanctuary reside

in one of the forgotten languages,
those spoken by drunkards & cattle,

those prisoners of war, those who know

there is no such thing as a bad day when
you have the doorknob on your side of the door.

She says my brother's twin died at birth
so for years he is half a self. She says

this man is my uncle. She says she's
coming to get me on that front porch

for hours where my father locked
his daughter, too terrified of

the power of my want to be kind,
a funnel cloud that could swallow

those who know the house is alive, those
rooms that changed in sleep & I could

always find the secrets in the bedside
drawers. She says no, she was one of

those who live in the forest long enough
to know where the gold is buried.

those lost, those anonymous, those dream-singers,

those who sit through the piercing test for life in Christ's side.
As in stigmata, the part of the pistil that receives the pollen,

9) the portion of a body that can withstand the hard pew
& after church, my grandfather prying the knife

from our drunken neighbor's hands & the man weeping
on his knees to the howl of sirens. O the nature of love,

the sideways glance. Few jealousies liquor can't cure for

those who suffer nostalgia, the pain of return. They forget
past lives & so hungry for any history come willing

again to her banks, cup their hands to their mouths—
Here's to irony. In this life, no amount of drink will erase

those wives in church clutching their hankies, their purses, their children.
You know the women who hold onto the world like this.

They've married the wrong man, taken the wrong job,
walked down the street during the hour of wolves.

No white-knuckled embrace can save them, no good deeds,
no casseroles left steaming on porch steps.

Include here:

those who would be labeled cannibals, those who cause shipwreck,
those bearers of bad news. those in love affairs with God himself,
those who see his face in everything,

Canisters bent with rust bearing labels of the old brands,

swollen tomatoes at the grocery—

[O my promise. To move into my wilderness & never return.

Dipped fingers in that melted wet pool of love a girl does

full of sorry, marked as I was. I slept in an attic across

from the man who broke me, that square of light

& how it framed the carrying-grief. In a small space

you get used to bodies, the famed bridge of his crooked nose

as he sat at his own window table. A prison cell endured for the day

he took his mother down the porch steps & beat her

while the neighborhood watched. And we watched as he beat

our mother with a fist the size of our heads at birth.

Include here:

those rationalized, disbelieved, despite clutching & prayer.

those marked, the eyespot of a protozoan.

those nuns, tertiaries, monistics,

those who stood perfectly still while the branding iron pressed,
(archaic) 1580–1590, to tattoo.

those tarnished—

My grandfather dropped the knife & said: *They'll be coming for me.*
We are never safe—fingerprints tell more than one story.

In the living room weeks after the funeral, a streak of blood remained
on the wall, but it's nothing to claim. A line that divides any room

& anger—

I'm saying the neighbor opened his wife's neck. And something
came fluttering into me, into my chest, some alphabet about how to hold

a secret, write it down so no one would recognize the flap of skin,
the swirl that belongs to us as that bitter braid in the sky, the green air

that pressed on my mother wiping dishes, wishing the house
could fly anyway, take with it to the crashing shore

those buds opened prematurely, those initiates, those drinking at the banks

of the Mnemosyne, my arm reaching over the alleyway that split us,

strangling his throat through the open window.

                                    I did not believe,

                                            nor could I remember exactly.

Grandmother asked *He get to you?*

I went carrying a basin of water because that love,

so dull in its labor, so benign,

came too late, could not be real. She scrubbed the potatoes,

made the soup. She scrubbed the skin of my back with her rough hand,

parting my grief, agate-
shellacked. *He get to you, I said.*

O the tiny arcs of Mary's tears carved in gold relief—

O *Prisoner, My Stowaway, My Imposter*

It's raining in the desert. If every narrative contains
its own opposite. I am wet & you are a guest.

Or I *am* you,

a clump of blister beetles posing on the stem, a girl to the eyes
of the male bee grown stupid in his loneliness—

I know, I know. There there. It's everyone's mistake. She smells so good.

We cling to his belly in this angle of sky.
We tremble as he thrusts.

A horse in some pasture waits for sundown. She is no one
to me. I have done her no harm. I cannot fathom

I will pass her lips.

But when I leave there is a knot in his eye I can't unravel.

A rash on his skin, *an easy one
to make,* a plea-bargain

& he stows himself a baby in the back of my old station wagon
headed west & away.

We have chosen to mate. We make our way to the hive.

She smells so right, as when I was young, terrified of rain,
I buried my face in my mother's denim crotch—

Who will feast on these larvae? The sweet meat of the almost-honeymakers?

Who will stroke the nose of this horse as she inclines her neck
to the hay barrel?

Unless the gun is pointed at their heads, the heads of their children,
do they wail? Are they in the street wailing now? Who, I ask you, will wail?

I will. I left. I came through Blue Earth, Minnesota,
& lightning. My last sky opening.

I traveled the sheath
of a desire

that maimed, tried for the horizon & by afternoon
I was a stranger to some jackstraw

who watched with 3-D glasses all
I designed in relief.

An executioner who sipped on bourbon before he triggered me
with his finger in the cold night.

And I am insatiable. A not in his eye I knot, untie.
I sign my name Jane Doe, just-don't-know.

I turn south, having chosen so wisely between victim & outlaw.

To calm the erasure of my guilt a palimpsest: *I will stop*
at the next flash & offer you my breast,

But they harvest our clutching bodies in the alfalfa & feeding her
poison her, the quiver of canter lost like song.

And of course he knew all along it was you I was worrying,

that I wanted my own body. *Now what was the*
story you were telling as I cracked eggs?

I ask the window, this flower
laden with tricksters,

Who wails? Who traces
the way out?

those whose polar bodies collapse, including

the gravitationally-swooned-by-the-low-chug-of-cog-turning-
deep-in-the-earth, the asymptomatic-with-cataclysm. such

classification limited to those resigned to call the body
home. Two long needles pierce my thighs, pin me

to subtext, that which must be lifted to be held,
that which reading erases. My father's tender clench

on the chair before I count backward. Latex gloves
& sepulcher lights, a vast forgiveness of this violence

I will not recognize again for years. Refer to Art. 3
of the Geneva Convention. The wounded and sick

shall be cared for. To a wild thing, care is an insult.
I woke to that fluent & malnourished river, as in

8) what extenuating ghost moves in the veins, *(archaic)*
1375-1425—to emaciate, to reduce density—also *(geog)*

River Rouge, city in Michigan, pop. 9,917 at the 2000
census. Home to a coal-burning plant that pumps out

47,710 tons of sulfur dioxide—O river, my best wound.
Riveted to prairie. The smell of rotten eggs, berths of

those with yellow fever. those whose bones surface like fans,
including those fornicating in places where there is such mud,

Once you learn a word you find it everywhere, everyone
writes it on packages & billboards. If pain is warning

& pleasure incentive, what is the long burst of electricity
between fingertip & flannel nightgown, the sad baying

of dogs & merchants? Mornings in August I was sent
to pick raspberries or tomatoes in the fenced alley plot,

last of our land left among steel & steeples. My fingers
stained, newsprint & nectar. But neighbors can never

escape. The moment the sky conditioned a warrant
in a funnel of blue. As in, pay attention to this. As in,

my people split so I could see their doubleness cultivated
like a row of stitches wanting to seal something back, or

to remove the acid from my aunt's lungs, the long fibers
buried because her tree is not a sacred lamp we burn

on the front porch in rust falling from the sky. And
the labia of my cousin, excised to stop the malignant—

moment in which she buys a mirror & crouches over
her own cave & sees she will take the covenant of darkness

to her death—Here, I want to say, I will touch you among
what robins open & devour & shit the red disasters of

those who acknowledge the vanishing point of song that catches
in the choir's throat the exact moment they know no escape,

those who care for every little piece of the earth they encounter,

As in putting a flame to this wick for you who collapsed
with me. As in silence my lover goes down to discover

the jagged clitoris still begging for love. As ineluctable
as my untried hand to my aunt's broken face—my want

to touch all of this as this opening is always the virgin
mother, arms spread, taking me into her brined robes.

those who shimmer in corn spell, those with hearts

wide as watermelons, those who know me, those who listen
with ears made of conch shells, I am your own foundling.

That is to say, a throwaway you've gathered considering
many are raped by the gods & society is unkind, will not

furnish apartments for those who fulfill prophecies &
who can find such carbon-dating with a mother hovering?

Assign her any evil, but I am insistent when I want love—

those for whom denim pants are atrocity, those feral children.
The gazelle boy, stolen from his wilderness in 1946,

chased down by the hunters' jeeps, bound hand & foot.
Forever to dream of careening 50 mph in the Syrian desert,

a storm of sand & ass-divot. Once rescued, a beggar.
Men in the obfuscating street paid a quarter to watch

him race taxis until they chained him to the asylum wall,
his legs aching & as if it were another planet, never again

a face like hers as he approached her in the grasslands—

those isolated, those Dryads, the girl captured by loggers
who kill the spirit in trees. Then claimed by her father

for the long scar, that mark of flesh that survived the depth of the Cambodian jungle for 19 years. She will not eat

with chopsticks, glances left to right, right to left, awaiting
the moment of her escape. And the other story hidden,

the raw flesh of her wrists, the man seen holding his machete,
the genocide, the Khmer Rouge, the 22 babies born & grown

without seeing another human being, so their textured faces,
so they can only fall in love with other trees, drink sap—

those suffering Kaspar Hauser Syndrome, psychosocial dwarfism,
mistakenly understood as failure-to-thrive. You learn over time

to take up smaller spaces when there is no competition,
when you are tied to your mattress. Your desire isn't growth,

but an invisibility clause. As in the Naderis, whose mother
was blind, whose father was given a hacksaw by the authorities

to cut the bars on his daughters' cages. The streets are a forest,
how you crave a walk with your mirror, division of cell—

those the wolves sing to sleep. For example, Shamdeo, who loved
the smell of blood, who ate the raw chicken entrails & all

just as the other four cubs ate. Or Djuma, who bit the oilmen
attempting to rescue him, whose mother, killed in the purge,

threw her body over his—The crash of Flight 255, 1987,
lone survivor Cecelia Cichan's mother wrapped her body

around the girl's chair to absorb the fire, the impact—

those monsters of sorts, those coming in the fury of love, those licked
& bathed by such tongues. Say what you will, my mother fed us

from her own breasts. They made her leave us on that farm.
The boyfriend's mother, riffing on Psammetichus's foray

into the Forbidden Experiment, however could not offer
a flock of sheep so we might learn to beg. She locked me

in the attic, my brother in the cellar. I peed in a flowerpot,
begging a snake plant back to life. And this was the one story

my mother could never bear, the crash of my gold desperation
on crumbled swords & grey soil. His voice echoing up the vent,

terrified of the darkness, the swallowing drain & my reply:
It's only just a few more hours. You can hold on till then—

those children imprisoned by Emperor Frederick II, 1211, to discover
the natural language of God, unuttered as this boy thin enough

to slip through chain-locks, this ghost willing to endure beatings,
riding past the devil who knits endlessly in her chair. This boy

creeps up the ladder to touch my fingers beneath the trapdoor.

[And if I get there before you do, I'll cut a hole the shape of you

leave you free to roam the wild territory of my heart,

this last fisted coral flaming beneath the waves,

a stone in the fields of the dead,

I'll cut a hole and pull you through,

Away from any voyeur who longs

to touch your cornsilk hair

fine with cobwebs

& soot—

And take the comb, a winnow, through—

O the tiny arcs carved in
gold relief.

those who covet the bridges in other cities,

for example, the Lost Pleiad, who ran from disaster,
her ruin formal as the hull of a crashing ship,

a borer in the axis. The duty to open. The 007.
The story of a man you can tell in a woman's face.

Amnesia of proteins, membranes, cytoplasm.
Promised coral the teacher brought for the feast

of the steel-children's eyes: dull, uncolored, skeleton.
One boy turns away, shuffles his feet, never recovers

those shivering on the deck, those who were once stars.
those for whom crumbling is not an instant's act,

a fundamental pause in which enlightenment:
a mother might sell herself. Her children,

penniless, cannot buy her. Nor can they bury her.
To bring any sea-farer inland is murder.

Disaster victims cannot sleep in white houses
built rows upon rows. The bottle before her

at the formica table for hours before she leaves

those who understand diatomaceous earth, as in
made of algae. And myzotrophy: 1) to suck

*those who seem, in the dark passageway, like they cannot
comprehend scars.* As in, he said my face looked like

money. Or, rupture 6) cause a breach & 7) suffer
any disease of horizon. That is, the room filling

with Zyklon B. And O the marvelous catacomb of
the body where time slows for each alveoli's evacuation,

*those who know every sale is an amputation. those who
can't sell & lose limbs anyway. those who take up*

*the thick knot & count protrusions. those who whisper.
those for whom single mausolea may be permanently sealed.*

*those consecutive & slow. those who long to be anywhere,
anywhere else.* Re: Nuremberg Document #NI-9912,

the Degesch Manual. Fix a sign with the legend.
In several languages. Mark with a death's head.

See Harmon: "warning indicators removed."
Variegated thud of 840 soaps falling to the floor.

those animals insane for the destination,

those who cannot pause at the horizon.
For example, my first lover's mouth,

the squeak of green tree clumsy & bold.
Everyone else kneeling

in church & his head on my thigh & the long groan of springs.
As if arranging. A dappled ring of flowers for sunrise.

For example, the tiger, whose skin.
That is to say, incantation.

As in gold & orange & black, of course.
As in honky-tonk bars where we pass the microphone indiscriminately.

those who are sockets,

including both those for whom the electrical impulse & those recipients,
3) (anat.) a hollow in one part for receiving another part, the concavity

of a joint. The dented bed in that attic, too, from generations of.
As to say, the birch tree outside the window that Sunday was

a perpendicular I rose to make, the parting of my thighs
still wet. And the hunger & lightning & heavy.

As in the steeple over which I hovered
& hovered until.

those who know rain, so long in coming, softens husks of corn.
those who crack eggs at a table once used for the slaughter.

As in the train that carried my grandfather home
& the flash of his axe that even a hog admired

ready with long wailing for the pasture's edge.
For example the yolks I gathered & split.

As in the cuttlefish, her Cassiopeian eyes, the bone
taken by jewelers, all things stolen we cannot replace.

As in the canary my mother buys so she won't be so alone
with this man who makes a sign with his fingers like "okay"

And flicks the bird in the face until it cannot walk or fly.
That is to say, wreaths, a circular band of flowers.

And the medicine of the tiger, who is hunted
& who cannot cure &

those who have no other choice,

As in she fills a pan with water,
holds the bird down.

As in the heartbeat slackens
against her palm,

those who croon, those out of work, those in an abandoned boxcar.
those who hold what can never die nor reach the border.

those who frequent carnivals,

caught in the rings of Saturn. Prickling
rinse cycle. The laundromat our only

escape from summer with mother
in this halfway house that forbids

those who are the product of a sour meeting
between egg & sperm—

                                    [but O how joyfully a
                                    membrane collapses!

So the undertaker nods, whispers:

Lucid, girl, to love your own breaking.
You'll never be disappointed again.

And: Yes, I see where you've been,
the limelight. They upheld you here,
praised your journey,

those who would do you no harm,
lamb, duckling,
turtle, dove.

                        Carbon of your existence
coats the bars of the crib where your teeth
came in gnawing.

Now a summer buried 8 years in, gangplank,
worm-hole, games beneath the covers,

those who play tennis with spatulas & balloons,

your brother's hot breath on your cheeks,
cramped thighs, sweat in every crevice so you

become the next person, hand over mouth,
quiet as the director creeps past the window,

(those who pray for an elephant to swallow them)

as if the body is not a landmine, a documentary:

She's got a waitress job, now, no man,
so she belongs to you wholly & brings you
borrowed books that pile on the bedside table,
opening the wideness of the foregone world.

As in 1) African sunsets & 2) the winnow of
grain, or 3) Laura Ingalls' father lifted his gun—

[O
that rankling
of desire

those who plug their ears in ancient buildings,
those who avoid pleas & moans coming through

the pipes & toilets. As in the method to please.
Tattling her arms around him at the door—

those who are prison-broken, those who allow
themselves to be lifted in expatriate arms, earn
pink wisps that melt on the tongue. those carnies.
1549—refer to the Italian *carnelevare,* to remove
meat, literally: *raise the flesh.*

                            That first relief
of *outside* on your smuggled skin so you drunken,
come to believe anything.

Ferris wheel lights
play on the vast ceiling of sky—

Run out of coins & you'll barter,
lean over the sticky counter (as if you are your own)
& in the sudden secret carnival language:

Just give me the chance.

                        Take aim as any young warrior,
                    keep the night going
with your desire for a clothespin
to chart the bliss of air, kiss the rim of an old milk bottle
& clunk into its center—

those who ride the spinning ride, those who cry when
the floor drops out, those who will never come clean,

those who have become boys protecting their mother,
those who walk on the map of Jupiter, those freaks:

That tent. The Ape-Girl or Encephalitic parts
the flap for your small head. They know you

are family. They see through clothes & skin.
And that prize clutched tight beneath your arm!—

O Buttercup. Poodle. Giraffe. Cuttlefish.
As if you can hold to any riches in this lifetime.

those dallying, dallying, wanting to go in,

those fruit flies on the edge of a wineglass, those who would be happy to die.
Some of us feel it so strongly we are children wrapped in years of flesh.

During underwater documentaries, coral bright as blood dripping
in the sink in the house where the crime—That year, the gold left my hair.

When a girl is *forbidden to eat turtle or turtle eggs.* The skin, like paper, crumpled.
A woman's skin always walks down streets, a thousand petals of burn.

Any day she could be swallowed by the radiation in her bones. This is how
one moment fills an entire life. *These flowers are beautiful, these eggs.*

They drop a bomb on a city where she has already let down her hair & wept.
She has already sung a husband goodbye. Where a rivulet spilled from a trough

& eddied in the slight morning breeze, so small, so very small she might
have imagined it. Nothing doesn't love a prison. We are greedy for time,

but we soon change our minds. My grandmother grabbed the edge of the skillet
& the skin, like paper, crumpled. The truth I might have told her written

there. (Once he stood up from my body to drink a whole glass of water
& his Adam's apple—I wanted to cut it from his throat.) But here, a breeze

on the back of our necks *during the season when the turtles are breeding* &
languages, languages murdered before those *cellmates gathered around such weeping,*

those for whom double-jeopardy, those pleas substantiated. Every prison offers
some measure of comfort. As in, movie night where our coral reappears.

And this: we'll never have to tell our story again. In the room with her body,
her heavy blue hand, we are left to love *those who free us from the binds we wanted.*

living must bury

A bird never recovers. I am young, then, dangerously
So. In love
& the uncertainty. Principal
moment in which

Knees between knees. Though we can't feel the roads
We are being. Blooded & paired,

Delivered, a crushing empathy reverses itself

Against the cage. A boulder falls & I grow around
That crush. Of my mossy ribs. I will sing the truth of roads.

To separate is to kill & every breath goes over

The edge. I pull fingertips against the prison stone. Where I crouch
As if
All my life. The pattern of my skin was re-
Moved to him & the gilded misplace.

In one story, the fish thrusts toward her flaying. I move to him.
Coming again & again. I swim. To the surface of the lake

I kiss & kiss. All I see,
But his mouth my own reflection & we disap-
Pear, pointing

Beyond the lapping signs. Of birth,

Where the bones bleached. The shape of his hand. Rising from the prairie,
Scripted by mustard seed, fallowed by my

Flight to any violent set. Of arms. Where the
Furniture gives histories. In another story we are making love

Beneath. We are the chairs in which we rest.
In which he strains toward my crouch.

Never recovers from first flight & yet recall
The pattern. Of my skin

Soaking up each acid arsenal
In the history of barter,

The hollow pound of anchor & flash
Of encoding bars.

We are not tigers as tigers

Must hunger & Hank Williams crooning to tables

We're so lonesome we could

Open the mouth of the paper dragon we've invented with crank
& weld. He sips his coffee. The tables cry out for our legs

Straddled & familiar. Beneath last agonies, peonies, my dying fetters
Flesh to any gravity & of the pear, the whetting

Again. Pull though we might at our appetite

We are bound. To the clip & tangle. The after in which.
I break the surface so briefly to find myself hunted & myself

The hunter. The sweet of this bite.
The muted & only abyss

To sing of the coming.

those who cannot reverse the damage of Armstrong's boots,

those barn cats having escaped fire, those who look
over their shoulder at every dry-grass crackle.

Agoraphobia, 1871, fear of the marketplace.
I sniff my own shirt to see who I was before

his ghost was fully dead & I came untethered,
refused to return no matter how I grasped

those who sat in church at seven years old screaming prayer
while God did nothing, God filing his nails, God whistling.

God glowering from his hospital bed. As in my grandfather
stared at me & saw his daughter's face & raged: *Wasn't*

it you, wasn't it you I come to get from that motel room
with some guy? Wasn't it? No need for a second storm

for us to take cover. After the first, we duck at every
stray breeze.

[O wasn't it me? A putting green for real grass?

Aren't the borders of flesh actually rivers, tributaries,
4-part harmonies? The salt of my eyes, the blood in

this river, in praise of this wound you go down for

those orgasms pulled from the center, long chain of vowels,

O,

O,

O

The tip shattered the moon's surface in an instant,
but then we knew what we looked like from far away

*those who take only the tusks, leaving behind the burden
of flesh, the grey & wrinkled hide—*

—O girl carved in steel & shackled in twining splinters,
were you once made of corn, of light?—

It takes an elephant eighteen hours to bleed to death.
A fish, ten minutes. Mirrored, twinned inside, I leapt

from my self & my landing destroyed:

*those without scars to recall the wound, those trophies,
those beating their tailfins against the headlines.*

those who hail semis, those seers, those canaries

blinded by lightning, those who start singing at midnight.
Girl, hardscrabble girl, mouth open & slack, walking

the highway's side. The gods blinded the Corn People,
too, because they were almost gods themselves, holding

weapons of mass-destruction, those lodged beneath
the sternum, encased in protein, lipids & fibrous matter.

Lips, teeth, tongue. Curses given over daily bread, etc.
Can't you see them, their dazzle-bright skin & tassel

as they come down the mountain, baskets balanced
on their heads? How shocked the first victims are.

those who find they survived. The cluster bomb
that exploded in Ali Mustafa's eyes was thief.

No one can find the star that holds his final vision—

—American soldiers, smoke, his brother's face, the stray stem
that insists on growing, elixir of green, *the beautiful uncut hair of graves*
in a place where there is nothing but death, & what he thought
was a toy—

those for whom the future sings even when it's gone blank,

Driving the back roads near my father's house I try
to lose myself, but my hands on the wheel lead me back

through corn home, where the pitchfork has no purpose
but my grief & my grief could not tire of a rusted plow

left in winter's field—The problem is hoping love
will save you. The problem is waiting for the rescue.

That is not God. God merely warns of the collapse,
flies off, trusts that some will get out in time

with words to tell the stories we need. But given just
one small sip, how can a seer undo his suffering

without mistakenly undoing buildings where people
wave flags in the windows? Without believing it's her

own'life she must undo? And what dirge shall we wail

for *those who did not come through?* Night of moon they
drop another bomb. It snows inside my empty womb

& his shirt over the line. I wake silent & take off
my nightgown to stand in front of the window.

I have no prayers except my barter with the next life:
I can close my eyes. But I know too much about the price

of redemption to wish for it, the will of the demon
to hold fast, the nature of the pill to uncure again &

centuries pass, no way to discern night from day.
They run their fingers through the brittle kernels

that once nourished, once were gold. The girl wraps
her leather tight around her, hails a semi, lights a smoke.

And the caverns, the mines, used-up, forgotten,
crumble & close, leave you to call out a warning:

those for whom the body is the same God they imagined as children.
It forgets nothing. It punishes. Unheeded, a white-hot cord

circles the throat.

I stand before the glass remembering
how we once made love in the day lilies & orange petals

                    fell into his hair.

O *You with a Spine*

O Gondolier pulling me through,

           who would work your mouth against this magic of mine,

this dank water & twinned, oared,

O Scarecrow you rise through grass at the roadside, Crucifix spine,
            [who would work your mouth]

O Doctor, these pills dissolved against cotton pocket stained blue, faint,
   like the first sky

the morning after, Bone column you memorize,

O Dog wearing a sunspot on the floor, Dreaming all the while of
   something common,

bread rising in a wooden dish on the stove,

O Leper, I have seen
you in marble, I borrow your spares

like light switches that lead to nothing because rain in December
            [against this magic of mine]
& the dog wears a sunspot on the floor,

gnaws the bone, O Water boils until the pot scars, O Rafters of the fallen barn
where they used to store their love in grain, I count every grain, O Gondolier

I count your mouths,

O Panhandler, O Heart, don't testify, You will certainly outweigh
a feather, O,

Your mouth a feather, O Feather, I have not stolen

bread, I have not, O Sunspot, O, Crocodile,

O Shepherd, O,

     O.

glorious, those excavators, hands that speak

in the night, move the earth, frozen, with stolen spoons.

You know by the edges of a man's mouth he'll last until dawn,
die, or labor endless for that glimmer—the open sky

brighter than cell walls & surface crumbling in the eye: O
face of the moon, too tired for shock. *Run, then.*

Resigned as *those who will not. Go.*

        those who fail to save themselves.

Peering at the broken gate for hours, as if solid & wrought

it is the snowy continent itself & entire, the hundred miles
you must walk to find the golden glow squared & sought

by all. One awkward step off, no way to return.
Aerial views show

        those off course, those well past, hands

held palm-face against the burn. Coming upon the fallen
they never doubt. Cover the eyes of the dead with snow

like their own tracks. *Poor bastard.* They lift their heads,
certain of their destination—

        You must insist upon the facts:

fire, warm soup, a woman's embrace. You know the distance
marks the depth of your desire & God notes such strife

& anyway, summer orchids will open, blood rushing out of
the earth's deep vein to sing to you alone in all this white.

Your life has chosen you out of all the others. Living kisses
you & whispers like a lover or your mother once made sure:

You don't need a church to pray.

But a sky equals freedom.
If only you'll keep moving, beat your heart. Open your fist

& take up a clot of floor. Don't listen for the guards.
If only you'll stray. Swallow. Swallow more.

those who dream in Matisses, those who travel

deep in the body & find a solitary color, those beyond religion.
Include here Ruth, the hybridization of love's decree & blessed

womb. As in 3) interior, which is to say further toward the center,
also *(geog)* a town in South Dakota, pop. 77 at the 2000 census,

where the city jail is 12 by 12. Also, *Department Of The.* Thus,
to protect something only until you find gold or the possibility

of fusion. Include here all political prisoners: Leonard, Assata,
Mumia. Revision: all prisoners are political prisoners. Clinging

to the iron bars at the P.S. on Normandie, L.A. County, where
98% of children qualify for free lunch, a boy knows exactly how

we crime hunger & how it gathers in the limbs, the creases, blue:
8) c. *to vanish into.* And peter, *(naut)* the flagged ship carrying

those leaving port, those with hankies pressed over their mouths,
those hiding in the coalbin, those who are told by history there is

a possibility of escape. But a city will press in on you, especially
in the days after you have your ticket & before the taker—

That is to say, the *blue devils.* Both despondency & the capsule
filled with barbiturate amobarbital or its sodium derivative, given

those who realize the ocean is a body. those who looked over the Badlands
& prayed the horses could make it. those who remember the mountains shifting,

their faces before the surgeons came in. those who see the nameless form
of a woman & love her in the morning, arm beneath a pillow, arching.

yes, those who fail to read guides & fall in love

with a woman's touch. Taken to this wilderness & forced to find a way,
we uncovered the tangled path
at each step. The skinning of a turtle's eye so to drink
the tart gel, the carriage of sacred bones in my braid & our clothes woven, too,
from the bark of trees, the sap of their veins & the honeyed pelts of prairie dogs,

those who rise singing from their dens. those who live under-
ground for long hours & are reborn & say a fleet of ships
is the loveliest sight on this dark earth.
                                        But I say it is what-
                        ever you desire.

        At first longing was merely survival,
3) the persistence of a trait & 7) persistence of the mouth in that triangle floe
she found first of necessity—
                Then, without warning,
    we unshackled ourselves from any labor
outside of this drinking & built a religion for hours
& the city faded until we slept & again
the rustle of pigeons,

those who moan as they nest in windows above the street, those mermaids in heat,
to persist as in to stay behind, as in smell. those who come into the room &
see they've left themselves in the sheets & must return to that hollow.

                        To unbridle,
1) to remove the bit from the horse's jaw, or 2) to un-
bride, to pull the gown from the scarred ribcage,
make shoes from nettle & larkspur, discover the muted but rainbowed
        crescents
of scales left on the linen & the outline of

those included in the present classification &
those sundry, derivative of syndrig, 1389.

As in separate, bordered by the skin,
5) a. the outermost layer of a pearl you grind between teeth for verification
of its time spent oystered, or 1) veneered with matched flitches
having a figure of concentric rings
& the lesser known: 2) b. the morsel removed as delicacy
from the pelvic hollow of a bird

& those who know what miracles birds know: every straight line misses a dark crevice
of branch. Not a one of us is spared. In every city a woman pauses
beside a window, her fingers barely touching the latch
as she lifts

everything & everything of her
I can carry
in my mouth or clutched beneath.

those shipfitters who dream

in perfect ships, hulls mad
with longing jut into blue or mist, depends.
On what you've lost. You think you can't bear it,
each clown uncovers himself in smiles the wider
the sadder. A girl's pulse a bracelet loosening her wrist.
A cup of coffee anywhere in the world on a warm porch,
or maybe yours is different. Your scars. I know that
after the burns small petals as a rose & pink
like I was then. Some evening comfort.
A river reaches up & tangles.
In Minneapolis the bridges like clamps
over the city's open heart stopped for winter.
In Dallas, the heat. You don't want to know Fort Wayne.
Can't know New Orleans. This same friend who saw you fall into love
sees you fall out. Sees you cheat. First thing in the morning
sinks his hands into dough, the baker. Discards the blood
in a long plastic tube, the nurse. Straps on a bomb.
The terrorist is lying, too. The friend who says
nothing is worth this. Everything is.

the last white night on this ship

If I can't be present, cannot be the one breathing here.
If I am numb as a laser.

Because someone on the same branch taught me to dig for fresh-water
    clams, to dissolve
dirt from their shells in oat water.

Because everything I swallowed was grit & now she is dying,

Keeper of secrets, the vowist.
Her cruel eye roves. In the white bed,

If any details of his time spent in prison remain, if a slogan in 5 o'clock
    shadow,
a knifed spleen. Or the exact spelling of his old name,

Was there someone on that boat like me, someone terrified?

At the edge imagining a field of stinking marigolds, that life would end
    at sundown

So never again vomiting breakfast into this sea, never facing the
    afternoon empty

of love below these decks the only thing that can save

This version of myself shrunken & caged, my face stitched together,
a nose vaguely familiar,

But is that mine? The way I might consider the tangle
of our bodies. Is this mine? This arm? This hip?

Waiting so desperately for the other shore, my true name, my crime.
Each sealed shell opens a moment to tongue the tossed grey water, secretly.

In photographs it's the Cadillac that tips me off, my mother's frilled dress,
everyone uncertain & smokestacks rising behind their proof.

Of a life well-lived, an accent hidden. Is this mine? Days my words elude me,

a step ahead in the fog. If your skin is too real, too infinite in the shower.

Why don't you turn around and hide it there? Why don't you step
off the plank?

those gathering the dust of the earth on fence posts,

those driving from Oklahoma, the clouds a woman swimming desperately
back to the canyon, her bruised arm reaching out. We were friends

with the children who lived in our house after, sung to sleep
by the same knots in the wood. But every prisoner seems a boy

to the enemy. The knife penetrates the sternum, light of lung, alveoli
where the conversion, looking out to sea from bow, drunk & miles lost,

my hands never forget her breasts. Standing in what had been the yard,
but without a house to tell. Photographs half-buried in mud. Mother

pulling her collar: *Want to see my scar?* _____. She opened
the cellar door, pushed us down. Loved us, beyond reason—

those last leaves that cling to the tree through January. My lover wished
she had been here at dawn to watch the sun slide slowly up the trellis

of our bodies twined. A boy dies of smallpox, his mother notes this
by dashing her head against a sharp stone, that is to say

those stars whose light might still be visible: a hand came into the water
which had been all sunlight & algae & broke a part of me for itself, stole

my color. *Cocktease*, she said, drawing the covers angrily to her chin.
Bleeding out of my throat, decimal point by diameter. No matter.

Energy collects in the non-space that comes between red & knife.
And life always folds back on itself at the place where it's halved,

so you'll endure everything twice, do the math of death,

those who climbed to the bottom of the old well to press their heads
against the cool walls. We relieved, unspeakable, that heat.

Then winter. That is, the small motel in South Dakota where
a woman works alone nights, rattle of the furnace in off-season.

I cut lemons for the water. They opened my mother's bird-throat
& two days later my grandfather drowned in his own blood.

They cut out what he made her keep & loosened, he returned
to constellation, particulate angst. They'll mine any organism

who cannot scream. Most hold genocide a *deliberate* policy,
he says—No one meant to annihilate _____.

The dank smell at the bottom when we realize she's never coming back.
Too late, the last hour, after he has ripped off her underwear & hurled them

into the pines, she finds the misplace of her voice, screams.
The tornado was the skeleton when you looked up into its cool dead eye.

Promiscuous as mercury. The air smelled of almonds just before
we lost everything, just before I went down on my knees for

those who evidence the violence done between souls,
dead bee on the pillowcase,

O the pollen

Notes

All "real" definitions and word origins from *The Random House College Dictionary, Revised Edition*, 1988, or the Online etymology dictionary: http://www.etymonline.com/

Statistics regarding the 2000 Census: http://www.census.gov

page 1:
Red wolf bounties: http://www.timberwolfinformation.org/updates/redwolf/info.html

page 4:
Reference to the following Galileo quote: "The sun, with all those planets revolving around it and dependent on it, can still ripen a bunch of grapes as if it had nothing else in the universe to do."

page 5:
From *Ode to Nightingale* by Keats: "She stood in tears amid the alien corn."

page 8:
reference to accounts of Virginia Woolf's suicide.

page 9:
reference to Rumplestiltskin

page 12:
Reference to "Bridges join but they also separate" from Jeannette Winterson's *The Passion*, Bloomsbury Publishing Ltd., Great Britain, 1987. p. 61.

page 14:
Prisoner of War quote from: http://www.humanevents.com

page 15:
The Lost, The Anonymous, The Dream-Singers is the title of a section of Muriel Rukeyser's *The Life of Poetry*, Paris Press, Ashfield Massachusetts, 1996. p. 90.

pages 24 and 33:
"in places where there is such mud" and "animal insane for the destination" refer to lines from the Sylvia Plath poem "Getting There."

pages 27 and 29:
"those with hearts wide as watermelons, those who know me, those with ears made of conch shells, those monsters, those coming in the fury of love" are references to "The Big Heart" by Anne Sexton. *Anne Sexton The Complete Poems.* Houghton Mifflin Company, Boston, 1981. p.462.

Information regarding the Forbidden Experiment available from www. feralchildren.com

pages 31 and 32:
References from poem 1010 by Emily Dickinson: "Crumbling is not an instant's Act/A fundamental pause" "A borer in the axis" "ruin is formal" "consecutive and slow." *The Poems Of Emily Dickinson, Reading Edition.* Ed. R.W. Franklin. The Belknap Press of Harvard University Press, Cambridge, 1998. p. 418.

"single mausolea may be permanently sealed" is from Wikipedia's article "Mausoleum."

Breaching German law, the Degesch Company, whose manual for standard uses of Zyklon B is often manipulated by Holocaust deniers to support their disturbing claims, manufactured Zyklon for the Nazis without warning labels and odorants, as Brian Harmon's paper "Technical Aspects of the Holocaust: Cyanide, Zyklon-B, and Mass Murder" suggests. He also demonstrates that "840" human beings could be killed by a single can of Zyklon, a statistic he uses to confirm figures deniers claim are impossible.

page 40:
"dallying, dallying, wanting to go in" is from Jorie Graham's "Self-Portrait As Both Parties" from *The End of Beauty.* The Ecco Press, New Jersey, 1987. p.14.

Turtle quotes are from a section of *The Golden Bough* by James Frazer entitled "The Seclusion of Girls At Puberty."

pages 46 and 47:
Margaret G. Zackowitz, *National Geographic*, February 2007: The New Jersey man's feathered patients ranged "from an inquisitive parrot who walked into an electric fan ... to a canary blinded by lightning" that "had to be taught to bathe and where to find its seed and water. Not being able to recognize daylight, the bird would often start singing at midnight."

Jonathon Steele in Baghdad, *The Guardian*, April 2003. "Clutching his mother's hand as he lay on a mattress, Ali Mustafa's head is half hidden by a bandage. He is a 'post-war' victim. The five-year-old was playing with his brother and two friends earlier this week when he picked up an odd round object. It was an unexploded cluster bomb, one of thousands that lie around Baghdad. It exploded in his hands, blinding him. His legs, scarred with shrapnel, will heal but Ali Mustafa's sight will never return."

"the lovely uncut hair of graves" is a Whitman reference, *Leaves of Grass*.

page 50 and 51:
Italicized portions from *The Book of The Dead of Nes-min*.

The title "living must bury" is from *The Heart is a Lonely Hunter* by Carson McCullers: "Why was it that in cases of real love the one who is left does not more often follow the beloved by suicide? Only because the living must bury the dead? [...] Or perhaps, when there is love, the widowed must stay for the resurrection..."

pages 56 and 57:
"say a fleet of ships is the loveliest sight on this dark earth. But I say it is whatever you desire" is a Sappho quote from *Poems and Fragments*, front matter, which however translates the line as "black earth" and "whatever you want." Hackett Publishing Company, 2002.

"those included in the present classification" is from Jorge Luis Borges *El idioma analitico de John Wilkins*.

Fence Books has a mission to redefine the terms of accessibility by publishing challenging writing distinguished by idiosyncrasy and intelligence rather than by allegiance with camps, schools, or cliques. It is part of our press's mission to support writers who might otherwise have difficulty being recognized because their work doesn't answer to either the mainstream or to recognizable modes of experimentation.

The Motherwell Prize is an annual series that offers publication of a first or second book of poems by a woman, as well as a one thousand dollar cash prize.

The Fence Modern Poets Series is open to poets of any gender and at any stage of career, and offers a one thousand dollar cash prize in addition to book publication.

For more information about either prize, visit www.fenceportal.org, or send an SASE to: Fence Books/[Name of Prize], New Library 320, University at Albany, 1400 Washington Avenue, Albany, NY, 12222.

For more about *Fence*, visit www.fenceportal.org.

Fence Books

THE MOTHERWELL PRIZE

living must bury	Josie Sigler
Aim Straight at the Fountain and Press Vaporize	Elizabeth Marie Young
Unspoiled Air	Kaisa Ullsvik Miller

THE ALBERTA PRIZE

The Cow	Ariana Reines
Practice, Restraint	Laura Sims
A Magic Book	Sasha Steensen
Sky Girl	Rosemary Griggs
The Real Moon of Poetry and Other Poems	Tina Brown Celona
Zirconia	Chelsey Minnis

FENCE MODERN POETS SERIES

Duties of an English Foreign Secretary	Macgregor Card
Star in the Eye	James Shea
Structure of the Embryonic Rat Brain	Christopher Janke
The Stupefying Flashbulbs	Daniel Brenner
Povel	Geraldine Kim
The Opening Question	Prageeta Sharma
Apprehend	Elizabeth Robinson
The Red Bird	Joyelle McSweeney

NATIONAL POETRY SERIES

The Black Automaton	Douglas Kearney
Collapsible Poetics Theater	Rodrigo Toscano

ANTHOLOGIES & CRITICAL WORKS

Not for Mothers Only: Contemporary Poets on Child-Getting
 & Child-Rearing Catherine Wagner & Rebecca Wolff, editors

A Best of Fence: *The First Nine Years*, Volumes 1 & 2
                    Rebecca Wolff and *Fence* Editors, editors

POETRY

The Sore Throat & Other Poems	Aaron Kunin
Dead Ahead	Ben Doller
My New Job	Catherine Wagner
Stranger	Laura Sims
The Method	Sasha Steensen
The Orphan & Its Relations	Elizabeth Robinson
Site Acquisition	Brian Young
Rogue Hemlocks	Carl Martin
19 Names for Our Band	Jibade-Khalil Huffman
Infamous Landscapes	Prageeta Sharma
Bad Bad	Chelsey Minnis
Snip Snip!	Tina Brown Celona
Yes, Master	Michael Earl Craig
Swallows	Martin Corless-Smith
Folding Ruler Star	Aaron Kunin
The Commandrine & Other Poems	Joyelle McSweeney
Macular Hole	Catherine Wagner
Nota	Martin Corless-Smith
Father of Noise	Anthony McCann
Can You Relax in My House	Michael Earl Craig
Miss America	Catherine Wagner

FICTION

Flet: A Novel	Joyelle McSweeney
The Mandarin	Aaron Kunin